WISDOM
YOU WON'T
DESPISE

LIFE LESSONS FROM
MOMMA AND DADDY TYLER

MAVIN J. TYLER

Scripture quotations marked (ESV) are taken from THE HOLY BIBLE, ENGLISH STANDARD VERSION®, Copyright© 2001 by Crossway, a publishing ministry of Good News Publishers. Used by permission.

Scripture quotations marked (KJV) are taken from the KING JAMES VERSION, public domain.

Scripture quotations marked (NIV) are taken from THE HOLY BIBLE, NEW INTERNATIONAL VERSION®. Copyright© 1973, 1978, 1984, 2011 by Biblica, Inc.™. Used by permission of Zondervan.

Scripture quotations marked (NKJV) are taken from the NEW KING JAMES VERSION®. Copyright© 1982 by Thomas Nelson, Inc. Used by permission. All rights reserved.

Printed by Prize Publishing House, LLC
in the United States of America.

First printing edition 2025.

Prize Publishing House
P.O. Box 9856, Chesapeake, VA 23321
www.PrizePublishingHouse.com

ISBN (Paperback): 979-8-9929954-0-4
ISBN (E-Book): 979-8-9929954-1-1

Library of Congress Control Number: 2025921495

The family unit is the backbone of society. There is something beautifully triangular and eternal about the uniquely special and unbreakable bond between a mother, a father, and a son. Something that death, nor life, nor time, nor space could ever tear apart. This phenomenon is powerfully captured by the author and seasoned law enforcement veteran Lt. Mavin Tyler in this loving tribute to lessons taught, lessons learned, lessons lived, and lessons loved. This is a master class in family values shared between these honorable parents and published by this resilient son for future generations.

Mr. Byron Parker, MSW, BSW, LCCA
Social Work Professor, Texas Southern
University, Houston, Texas
Association of Black Social Workers,
Houston Chapter, President
Coalition of Urban Resource Experts
(CURE), Founding Member

As Mavin's cousin, I read Wisdom You Won't Despise with both pride and gratitude. We share similar life stories — growing up, we both had speech impairments and received speech therapy, which sometimes led others to label us as less capable or not smart enough. His story is a heartfelt reflection of where we come from — a family grounded in faith, respect, and perseverance.

Through his words, I was reminded of the strength of our parents and the quiet lessons they taught us: to work hard, stay humble, and treat everyone with dignity. Mavin's journey from those early days in Pleasant Grove to the man he is today shows that true success isn't measured by wealth, but by the values we live by.

Wisdom You Won't Despise is more than his story — it's our story. It beautifully honors the legacy of faith, family, and wisdom that shaped us all.

A must-read for anyone who values timeless lessons passed down through generations.

- Derrick Bowens

Dedication

I dedicate this book to the late Mr. John Arthur Tyler and Mrs. Ann Tyler with a heart full of gratitude and love. Their integrity, faithfulness, hard work, and commitment to our family have taught me invaluable lessons that I am now able to share with the world. These teachings have been so powerful that without them, I would not be alive or where I am today. This dedication is my way of honoring their legacy.

I also want to thank my son, Mavin II, for his unwavering support and positive encouragement throughout the writing process. Also, during moments when I struggled to find the motivation to write, my daughter,

Laila, would remind me to finish my book so that the world could see it; her words meant a lot to me. Lastly, I would like to express my deep gratitude to my wife, Keisha. Her consistent support and unwavering belief in me have been instrumental in helping me stay focused and achieve my goals.

Contents

Introduction

HUMBLE BEGINNINGS

In a world that often celebrates the grand and glamorous, I have always found deep beauty in simple and peculiar things. My journey started not in the spotlight but in the quiet corners of a modest home filled with laughter, resilience, and wisdom passed down through generations. My parents, both remarkable yet humble figures, taught me invaluable lessons that have shaped my life more than any major accomplishment ever could.

I recall how the sun filtered through the kitchen window, casting a warm glow over the vibrant colors of the dinner preparations. The scent of home-cooked meals, the rich aroma of collard greens simmering on the stove, the sweetness of cornbread baking in the oven, and, of course, the fragrant spices that my mom always knew just how to blend, mingled perfectly with stories of perseverance shared around the dining table. Those were the moments when I felt the world outside melting away, leaving only the comfort and safety of home, a feeling I'm sure many of you can relate to.

The family room was our battleground, where intense card games unfolded in uproarious laughter and playful accusations of cheating. My older siblings would present their best poker faces, and I often felt a mix of pride when I won a hand or two against them. But it was in those games that I learned about friendly competition, strategy, and most importantly, the joy of bonding over shared experiences.

In a modest home with three bedrooms, as kids, we were tasked with keeping and maintaining our rooms with pride—a responsibility that sometimes felt overwhelming. Still, we knew it was a privilege to say we had a room we could call "mine." I recall the numerous battles I fought—not just against clutter, but also against my own procrastination, which led to my parents' frustration and serious consequences for a child at the time. My parents instilled in me the belief that keeping a tidy space leads to a clear mind. Although I struggled to uphold this idea, each reminder to clean served as a reminder that our home was a sanctuary. Later in life, I learned the importance of taking care of my belongings, but as a child, it was a difficult concept to grasp.

Financial issues loomed like dark clouds, ever-present, but every so often, a silver lining would break through. It was during our most challenging moments when little miracles occurred—unexpected checks, generous favors from neighbors, or, as my mom would say, a financial breakthrough. I learned early on that material wealth was not the measure of our richness. In Matthew 6:31-33, Jesus spoke of a provision that extends beyond physical needs, reminding us to seek first the kingdom of God, and all else will be added to us. In my sheltered view, we never lacked anything that truly mattered. Looking back, I realize I rarely noticed our struggles because love and joy filled our home, drowning out fears with laughter and unity, instilling in us a sense of hope and optimism. My parents offered me something far more precious than riches: a foundation of faith and resilience that would guide my journey, a lesson that continues to inspire me.

My dad, Mr. John Arthur Tyler, stood tall and proud, his presence both comforting and formidable. A lean, dark-skinned Black man with a mustache reminiscent of Carl Weathers, he commanded respect with his old-school demeanor. Clad most days in a blue jumpsuit and sturdy black work boots, he was a symbol of diligence and strength. His story began in Fort Worth, Texas, where he graduated from high school and was quickly drafted into the military during World War II. On the U.S.S. Missouri, he witnessed history, standing witness to a peace treaty that would change the world. Once he returned home, he built a legacy of hard work, spending 35 years as a postman without ever missing a day of work, epitomizing dedication.

My mom, Ann Tyler, was his perfect complement. With her curvy, doll-like figure and a smile that could light up any room, she brought an elegance that seemed radiant against the backdrop of our modest life. There was a captivating mystery about her, a class act through and through. Despite the

20-plus years that separated their ages, their love and partnership transcended societal norms; it was a beautiful testament to the unexpected ways in which love can manifest.

It's important for me to share that my father was a widower before meeting my mother. My dad had seven children from a prior marriage, my mom had two kids from a prior relationship, and my mom and dad had two children together, including me. However, many people might question the dynamics of such a blended family. Our family's story stands as a testament to the power of love, resilience, and the unexpected ways life can bring us together.

Through my parents' teachings and experiences, I learned that life's most valuable lessons often come in simple forms. Their sacrifices and hard-earned wisdom became my guiding light, showing me that greatness can grow from the smallest beginnings. They taught me the importance of hard work, family, resilience, and humility. Their humble origins and the lessons they've shared continue to inspire me today, and I hope they will inspire you as well.

In this book, I invite you on a journey through the life lessons I've learned, framed within the context of my incredible parents and the rich experiences we've shared. The first half will explore the powerful teachings of my dad, the embodiment of relentless determination and resilience, and the lessons he passed on to me. The second half will reflect on my mother's nurturing wisdom and the lessons I learned from her, focusing on the everlasting values she instilled in me.

Together, we will explore how the roots of humility and hard work can not only provide a solid foundation but also help us reach beyond our wildest dreams. Join me as we explore the stories and lessons that have shaped who I am, encouraging you to appreciate the beauty of your humble beginnings.

By understanding and valuing where we come from, we can better steer where we're headed. The wisdom from our parents is crucial to our success and growth. Solomon, who in my opinion was the wisest king ever to walk this earth, stated in the book of Proverbs, 1:8-9, NIV, "Listen, my son, to your father's instruction and do not forsake your mother's teaching. They are a garland to grace your head and a chain to adorn your neck."

Lesson 1

RESPECT OVER MONEY

I was born and raised in Dallas, Texas, in a small part of Southern Dallas called Pleasant Grove. During my childhood in the early to mid-1980s, Pleasant Grove was a warm and inviting community, bustling with families who shared common dreams and struggles. My dad, a dedicated postman, managed to buy our three-bedroom house with two bathrooms and a two-car garage, just a block from an elementary school. Moving to Pleasant Grove felt like hitting the jackpot for my parents, who wanted to create a nurturing environment for our growing family.

Our home was more than just a structure; it symbolized our collective effort and determination. In a world where earning a single income was often a struggle for Black families, my father's ability to secure a comfortable home for us was a source of great pride. The neighborhood was a tight-knit community, with everyone doing their part to ensure that our small corner of the world thrived. We were not just neighbors, but a family united by shared values and aspirations, a part of a larger story that we all helped shape. This sense of unity and shared purpose made us feel connected and part of something bigger than ourselves.

Respect was not just a concept we were taught, but a way of life we lived. If I or any of my friends got caught "cussing," any nearby elder had the authority to gently but firmly correct us, and we respected that.

There was no debate; instead, there was an understanding that elders should be honored. Their influence was profound, shaping our behavior and attitudes, instilling in us a deep sense of respect and reverence. Their role in forming our community values is impossible to overstate.

Our days were filled with adventure, but they also brought challenges. Mothers exchanged recipes, sharing both knowledge and love through the dishes they prepared. Neighbors lent each other essential items, such as sugar, eggs, and milk, as we all worked to make ends meet. Despite the hardships we faced, there was a strong spirit of resilience in Pleasant Grove. We were a tapestry woven with threads of rich culture, community, and determination. Our ability to overcome these challenges and thrive was a testament to the strength of the human spirit, serving as a source of inspiration and hope for us all.

Back then, technology wasn't as embedded in our lives as it is today. We didn't have cell phones, tablets, or the internet, and most families didn't even own a computer. Instead, we depended on sets of encyclopedias, those thick volumes of knowledge that lined our bookshelves. To us, they were the equivalent of Google, a resource for answers to questions that seemed to come up every day. Whenever curiosity struck, we were more than willing to dive into those pages and explore the world.

Our entertainment came from simple pleasures. We gathered around gaming systems like the Atari and later, the Nintendo. Atari came alive with Ms. Pac-Man and Space Invaders, games that were as challenging as they were fun. In the world of Nintendo, we found ourselves lost in the vibrant realms of Mario Brothers, Donkey Kong, and The Legend of Zelda. Tecmo Bowl and Punch-Out!! kept our competitive spirits alive as we cheered each other on during epic gaming sessions.

Let's be honest: buying a gaming system wasn't cheap. A Nintendo in the early 80s cost around $180. For a family of six living on a single income of about $15,000 a year, buying a gaming system was just a dream. However, we did eventually get one, but that story is for another lesson later in this book. Most of our time was spent outside playing touch football in the street—if you ran onto the grass, you'd be tackled. We played every sport imaginable and enjoyed games like "IT," a tag game, and couldn't finish the evening without playing "hide and seek." Those were some fun days. Those were days when our worries were minimal, and our dreams were vast.

However, every coin has two sides. The dark side of growing up in a vibrant and thriving neighborhood was hidden nearby, and a storm started to approach our community. The Crack Epidemic struck Pleasant Grove hard, turning our lively streets into silent corridors filled with despair. Addiction crept into our neighborhood, undermining the core values we cherished—respect, community, and support that we had cultivated over the years. The impact of the Crack Epidemic was profound, and it altered the fabric of our community in ways we could never have anticipated.

The once calm streets that echoed with joy and respect turned into silent shadows of addiction. Respectable mothers started walking the streets, lowering themselves by offering their bodies for sex in exchange for a few dollars. Meanwhile, fathers, who were once the protectors and pillars of the Black community, became figures that people feared and looked down on, instead of being honored and respected. This transformation was not just a change in perception but a deep shift in the roles and identities of these men. At the same time, some became addicted to crack and were no longer seen as the respected men they once were, but rather as individuals who were referred to as "crackheads."

I could see the changes in my friends and neighbors. Mothers, once proud and strong, started seeking comfort in the streets. Meanwhile, fathers shifted from protectors to shadows of their former selves. Our young people desperately needed guidance; without it, they were left to navigate dangerous waters alone.

During these times, our young people desperately needed guidance and direction, but that support was no longer accessible to many in my community. Without guidance and a strong male presence in the home, survival became a formidable challenge, leaving young teenagers to fend for themselves. As the epidemic escalated, drug dealers with cold, calculating eyes began to embed themselves deeper in our community, exploiting the vulnerable and desperate. Their whispers spread through the streets like wildfire. Many childhood friends I once played with fell victim to the epidemic, either becoming drug dealers or addicted to crack cocaine. The crack trade became a twisted lifeline for some, weaving dark threads into the fabric of our lives.

The wealth these dealers had was incredible; they moved around with a level of luxury that was hard to comprehend. They flaunted the finest jewelry, the most stylish clothes, and drove luxury cars, including Mercedes, BMWs, and Cadillacs. The temptation to get involved in the cocaine trade was within reach, but amid all this, there was someone who stayed unaffected by the appeal of material things, and that was my dad. In a community where many succumbed to the epidemic, my dad, Mr. John Arthur Tyler, remained strong and upright, a symbol of respect and resilience.

I had only a vague understanding of what respect meant at the time. Still, naively, I linked respect to those who had money and perceived power. Money and material possessions seemed to drive my community, and people with wealth often appeared to hold real power. As a young kid, it was easy to think drug dealers and hustlers were living the American dream. Let's face it, the American Dream, as portrayed by the media, was all about material possessions and wealth. But most people in my community weren't living the American dream; they were trapped in an American nightmare. Malcolm X captured the disparity between the American dream and reality for Black people in this country during the civil rights movement. He pointed out that while many people chase the American dream, most Black folks have only experienced the American nightmare. During this time, particularly during the crack epidemic and the surge in gang activity in my neighborhood, it certainly felt like an American nightmare.

In the middle of this American nightmare, there was a glimmer of hope, and that hope came from my dad and what I learned about the true value of respect. I can still vividly recall this moment: it was a Sunday afternoon after church during the summer when I was 10 years old. My dad, a pillar of strength and love in our family, asked me to walk to the store to buy a bag of ice and a few packages of Kool-Aid. These simple items were to be the refreshing complement to our delicious Sunday dinner. When I asked him if he would come with me, he surprisingly agreed! I never told him, but whenever I went to the corner store, I often faced uncomfortable encounters. Crackheads and different individuals would constantly ask me for money, and sometimes female solicitors would proposition me for sex in exchange for the few dollars I had. At just 10 years old, I was completely naive and hadn't been exposed to sex or the slang words related to it; I was as "green" as they come.

One time, while walking to the store, I encountered a female prostitute whom I'll refer to as "Ms. Head" for this story. She looked to be around 40 to 50 years old and certainly didn't resemble a supermodel. She appeared quite unkempt. Her skin was very dry, and her clothing—a yellow halter top and lime-green shorts—looked dirty and dingy, giving off an odor that suggested she had been outside for days without bathing. Her hair was disheveled.

As I was entering the store, she approached me and said, "I'll give you some head." I looked at her, confused and unsure of what she meant. She then explained her request by gesturing toward my private parts and mimicking the act with her hands in front of her mouth. I gave her a confused look and walked past her. This incident, along with other uncomfortable situations, sparked my curiosity about how my dad would handle such encounters. I didn't know what to expect on this walk, but unknowingly to me, I was about to embark on an experience that would change my life forever.

Pops walked into my room and told me we were about to go to the store. I quickly jumped up, grabbed my basketball, and looked at my dad with a sneaky smile. Keep in mind, I'm excited to see how my dad will handle all the chaos happening in the hood. As we were leaving, my dad grabbed his Coca-Cola baseball cap, and we were on our way.

As we were walking down the street, a couple of patrol officers stopped and waved at us. One officer pulled over and greeted my dad with a friendly vibe, even offering to play ball with me someday. Those same officers suddenly ended the conversation and went to an emergency call. Yep, you guessed it—they rushed to the corner store. We kept walking a bit further and came across a homeless man whom everyone usually made fun of. He was an older Black man, approaching us and asking for money and food from everyone he met. His clothes were filthy, and he had a full beard that looked unkempt. His hair was messy, as if he hadn't had a haircut in years, and he wasn't wearing any shoes. My first impression was that he was either homeless or struggling with drugs. I had seen him several times, and most people either ignored him or waved him off.

As my dad and I approached the guy, I saw his face light up with excitement when he saw my dad. My dad greeted the homeless man by saying, "Hey, Mr. Johnson, how are you today?" They hugged like they were brothers. I found my dad's interaction with Mr. Johnson quite strange, given that people like Mr. Johnson are usually treated as misfits. After they exchanged pleasantries, we continued our journey to the store. As we approached the rear parking lot of the store, who did we see? Yep, you guessed it again: "Ms. Head." I noticed he saw her and instantly asked her how she was doing and if she needed anything from the store. "Ms. Head" smiled and stated, "I'll take a bottle of Coke." My dad responded and said, "Sure, no problem; I know it's hot out here."

As we approached the entrance of the corner store, this spot was "lit." Cars were parked everywhere, and music was blasting. To our surprise, we walked right into a drug bust. I saw one of the neighborhood drug dealers, someone I had looked up to, being handcuffed along with other dealers. The same officers who had been very friendly with my dad had the guy I thought held all the power and respect on his knees in an inferior position, making him look weak and powerless. Despite having a lot of money, he was treated very differently from my dad.

Amidst the chaos, my walk to the store felt completely different this time. As we entered the store, the clerk noticed my dad and instantly greeted him by saying, "How is it going, Mr. Tyler?" My dad responded, "What's happening, brother?" We began searching for the Kool-Aid packages and other necessary items for the house. As you can imagine, I had a few questions for my dad about our encounters with the police, Mr. Johnson, and Ms. Head. However, I got a little distracted because I saw some candy. Pops said, "Pick out any piece of candy of your choice." I chose a Nutty Buddy, wafers with peanut butter sandwiched between them. Along with the items we bought for our home, my dad picked up some classic black flip-flops for Mr. Johnson and a soda for Ms. Head. When we reached the cash register with all these items, the clerk, whom I later learned was the owner, scanned everything for checkout. Then the most surprising thing happened: my dad reached into the back pocket of his work jumpsuit and realized his wallet was missing. The clerk noticed that my dad did not have his wallet, and before my dad could say anything, the clerk offered to let him take all the items and pay him back next time. I was shocked by this gesture. My dad showed immense gratitude, and they smiled at each other as we collected our items and left the store.

As we left the store, he handed Mr. Johnson the flip-flops, and Mr. Johnson had a memorable reaction. He smiled, thanked my dad, and started dancing. It looked as if he were running in place.

Ms. Head approached my dad, and he gave her the soda pop he had promised. She smiled and said, "Thank you, sir." He embraced her and said, "God has something special in store for you." I remembered her face; she looked at my dad with pride, which was unusual for someone in her position. It was truly something special to witness.

As we were walking home, I asked my dad, "Why were you so friendly to Mr. Johnson?" I didn't understand at the time because people who resembled Mr. Johnson were often mistreated, usually by drug dealers. He responded by saying that Mr. Johnson is our brother, and everyone, regardless of their social status, deserves respect. I had heard the word 'respect' before, and I knew to show respect to certain people, such as adults, teachers, pastors, and respected members of our community. However, when I saw my dad show respect to Mr. Johnson, who I later learned was a homeless drug addict, it changed my perspective.

That experience influenced how I treated people from that point on. I started to observe how people interacted with my dad, and it was impressive. Not only did he show respect, but he also earned respect from everyone, including police officers, gang-bangers, community leaders, prostitutes, and more. It was incredible to see my dad so highly respected.

Some people might say that giving respect to others is simply a natural thing. However, I disagree. According to Social Learning Theory, developed by Albert Bandura, people learn by watching others. We can learn positive behaviors from teachers, coaches, pastors, and especially our parents. On the other hand, we can also learn from negative experiences, such as those involving gangsters, pimps, and hustlers. Sadly, in many neighborhoods, people are often drawn toward these negative influences.

Today, disrespect has become common in many communities, including urban and suburban areas. It is not unusual to see children cursing in front of adults, people exchanging verbal insults, and individuals stealing from one another; the list continues.

I believe respecting people from all walks of life is a learned behavior that should start at home when children are young. In the New King James Version of the Bible, Proverbs 22:6 states, "Train up a child in the way he should go, and when he is old, he will not depart from it." This verse highlights the importance of teaching children to do what is right; the lessons learned will stay with them throughout their lives. However, if you are teaching or, more importantly, modeling bad behavior, those negative traits may also stay with your children as they grow older.

Reflecting on my own life as an adult, more than 30 years later, after witnessing my dad's encounter with Mr. Johnson, the officers, "Ms. Head," and the owner of the corner store, I have developed firm convictions about showing respect to everyone from all walks of life. Furthermore, when a person learns to show respect, they naturally build self-respect, making it easier for others to respect them in return.

I would like to emphasize the importance of showing respect to everyone. When you "give" respect, little do you know, you are planting a seed into the world. Galatians 6:7-8, NIV states, "Do not be deceived: God cannot be mocked. A man reaps what he sows. The one who sows to please his sinful nature, from that nature will reap destruction; the one who sows to please the eternal spirit will reap eternal life."

My dad always used to tell me that nothing is new under the sun and that laws govern our lives. I thought he was talking about our government. But he went deeper, referencing the laws in the Bible as the most important laws we should follow. Pops told me that if you follow our biblical principles and laws, then the government laws would be easy to follow. As I grew older, I realized my dad was correct.

My perspective changed during that short walk to the store on that Sunday afternoon, where I realized respect is far more valuable than money. In fact, because of the respect my dad had, he didn't need money that day at the store. Oh, by the way, Pops kept his word and paid the money back, but there's no doubt that respect truly holds more value than money.

Though adversity knocked at our door, I held onto the lessons from my early years. Our community's spirit had endured many storms. Because some members refused to give in to this evil epidemic, we, as a community, continue to stand by those same values and pass them on to our children. As I navigated those challenging times, I held onto the memories of our shared laughter, respect, uplifting words we exchanged, and resilience, drawing strength from the childhood that shaped me.

Pleasant Grove wasn't just the place I grew up; it was a foundation of my identity, a mix of childhood dreams and tough realities. It also served as a reminder that even in the darkest times, the fabric of community could still be sewn with threads of hope, respect, and mutual support. As I reflect on those days, I realize that the power of respect is far more powerful than any epidemic. An epidemic, money, and material possessions will come and go. But respect will endure even after we are gone from this earth.

I challenge you to prioritize respect for yourself, your fellow brothers and sisters, and your neighbors, and to be intentional in how you treat people. I believe you will see the powerful impact this can have on your community, church, workplace, and most importantly, your home, which will be cherished for generations to come.

Lesson 2

FINISH WHAT YOU START

Growing up, my dad, a figure of wisdom and guidance, had a unique way of turning everyday moments into valuable life lessons. One evening in mid-November, when I was about 11 years old, he decided it was time for me to learn the importance of finishing what I started. Little did I know that he would teach me that lesson in a way I would never forget.

My dad always took care of the yard by himself, making it look easy. Occasionally, I would come out to help, but he never forced me to stay the whole time. He noticed that when the job became difficult, or I got bored, I would stop helping and start playing around, channeling my energy elsewhere. He told me I was developing a bad habit, but at that time, I didn't see it that way. I was like any other 11- or 12-year-old who thought they knew everything. His patience with me, even when I didn't fully understand his lessons, was a testament to his wisdom in understanding that he was just planting a seed. He knew one day, all these lessons would help me in the long run, and he was right!

One Friday evening, I approached him about the leaves scattered all over the yard, expressing my concern about how unappealing it looked. I said, "Dad, the yard is looking jacked up." He paused for a moment before replying, "I think it's about time you take care of the yard for the family. I'm a little under the weather, and I need you to pick up the slack." I looked at him, considering how daunting the task would be, and then impulsively said, "Aw, Pops, that's nothing; I'll start on it tomorrow morning and knock it out." He smiled and reminded me that the bags were in the garage, and the rake was in the backyard, adding, "You must complete the front yard, backyard, and both sides of the house." I responded with an uncertain, "I got it."

When Saturday morning arrived, I walked into the kitchen to find my dad reading the newspaper. He had already prepared a breakfast sandwich for me, consisting of two pieces of toast with bacon and scrambled eggs in between. As we sat at the bar, he encouraged me, saying, "You can do it," with a serious expression on his face. It then dawned on me that I had committed to doing the yard work, and suddenly, my stomach started to ache. If you're thinking that I didn't want to do the yard, you're right; the thought of the work ahead was overwhelming. But his words of encouragement somehow made the task seem more manageable.

I hoped he would forget and handle it himself, but he looked at me and said, "I've got the rake for you, and I left everything you need on the front porch." I took a deep breath and finished my breakfast. After eating, I went outside, only to find it extremely windy and a bit cool as well. I knew raking leaves in these conditions wouldn't be ideal.

As I stepped outside into the gusty wind, my heart sank further. The trees were still full of leaves, which meant my task was far from over. I glanced over at the garage where the bags were waiting, but the thought of tackling the yard started to feel like climbing a mountain. Still, my dad's expectations loomed over me, and I didn't want to let him down. I grabbed the rake from the porch, the cold metal biting into my hands, and slowly made my way to the front yard. As I started raking the leaves, the wind danced around me, turning what should have been a simple task into a frustrating challenge. Leaves flew back into the areas I'd just cleared, mocking my efforts. I quickly realized that completing this job wouldn't be as easy as I had imagined.

As I was raking the leaves, a couple of my friends walked up and saw me in the yard. They both had remote-controlled cars that they were playing with. I remember looking at them like they were lucky and had it made in the shade! They jokingly told me I was working harder than a Hebrew slave. I gave them a look of frustration and asked for their help. They both looked at me like I had stolen something from them and said at the same time, "Hell naw!" They walked off laughing at me, saying I would never finish, and then they went on to enjoy their Saturday afternoon.

I continued with my task, which, in my opinion, was an impossible one, and with every few rakes, I felt like giving up. I remembered my dad's words about commitment. This wasn't just about raking leaves; it was about seeing something through until the end, no matter how hard it got. I could feel my dad's presence guiding me, reminding me that hard work often yields greater rewards. As I kept raking, I started to find a rhythm. The more I worked, the less intimidating the task became. I made small areas of progress, clearing patches of leaves that were once dense and overwhelming. Each pile I formed felt like a small victory. I saw my dad watching from the bedroom window, his eyes encouraging, a quiet reminder that he believed in me. On top of that, my mom came outside, pulled up a chair, and watched from the front porch. She saw the frustration in my eyes and my discouraged disposition and told me how proud she was. Her presence alone made me feel like I had a million spectators cheering me on.

After what seemed like an eternity, I finally finished the front yard and moved to the backyard. By this point, the initial resentment I had toward the task had transformed into a sense of accomplishment. I felt proud of sticking to my commitment. With every bag I filled, I realized the value of hard work and perseverance. The shift from resentment to pride was a testament to the power of perseverance and personal growth. However, it was late evening, and there was no more time to play with my friends or do anything I wanted for myself. I was a little disappointed about that part. The most satisfying part of this task was stepping back from the house to admire my work; the yard looked neat and presentable, just as I had hoped. Just then, my dad stepped outside, a wide grin spreading across his face. He beamed at the sight of my hard work, and at that moment, I realized that the lesson I learned that day went deeper than raking leaves. It was about responsibility, effort, focus, and the importance of keeping my word. "Wow, you really knocked it out of the park!" he said, giving me a supportive clap on the shoulder. His pride filled me with warmth, and I could feel the weight of my earlier disappointment begin to lift. As we walked back to the house together, a comforting silence enveloped us. I felt a deep sense of gratitude toward my dad, not just for the encouragement he gave but for the way he taught me these invaluable lessons. They weren't just applicable to yard work; they echoed through every facet of my life. In the years that followed, those lessons stayed with me. They guided me through school, motivating me to persevere through long nights of studying and difficult courses. When I pursued fitness goals, I remembered the satisfaction of completing a task and the discipline it demanded. Chores, work tasks, and even building relationships became manageable with that one simple lesson: keep pushing forward, no matter the cir-cumstances or distractions. The ripple effects of that day changed my perspective, making me see challenges as opportunities rather than obstacles. Much like raking leaves in the wind, I learned that sometimes persistence and focus can create something beautiful out of chaos. Looking back now, I realize that my dad's simple lesson still influences my daily life, shaping how I approach goals and com-mitments. Every achievement, from earning my degrees to nurturing my friendships, mar-riage, and more, is a testament to that eve-ning, a reminder that true satisfaction comes from the effort we put in and the promises we keep to ourselves and others.

Lesson 3

NEVER COMPROMISE YOUR VALUES

Growing up, my dad was more than just a father; he was also a mentor and guiding light. He had a way of weaving life lessons into our daily activities, and one lesson that stood out the most was the importance of never compromising my values.

When I was around sixteen, I faced a challenging situation that put these lessons to the test. A group of my peers began experimenting with drugs, and the pressure to fit in was palpable. One evening, as I sat at the dinner table, I decided to open up about it. My dad looked at me, his brow furrowed in thought.

"Son," he said, "it's easy to give in when everyone else is doing it. But ask yourself, what do you value? Your health? Your friendships? Your future?" He explained how drugs might seem appealing at first, but they could lead to a lifetime of regret. "Never compromise your values, son," he reminded me.

The pressure to use drugs didn't happen just once; my friends kept trying to tempt me even after they saw I was pulling away from them. Eventually, they approached me with drugs again. The Bible says in James 4:7, KJV, "Submit yourselves therefore to God. Resist the devil, and he will flee from you." This scripture proved true for me. I kept resisting, and eventually, they left me alone. I learned that standing firm might mean missing out on fleeting moments or people I thought were friends, but it also meant protecting my integrity.

As I progressed through high school, I began to observe how relationships work. I noticed some friends changing their beliefs and values just to please others. My dad, who always paid attention to my behavior and noticed my interest in girls, pulled me aside one day and said, "Never compromise your values, and always respect and protect your partner." He continued, "A partner should uplift you, not bring you down. Always choose the one who appreciates you the most." He shared stories from his younger days about how he walked away from relationships that didn't align with his values. His words resonated with me and helped me set boundaries to protect my heart. I encountered a few young women who didn't really value me; they only paid attention because I was persistent and went above and beyond to impress them. Through my experiences,

I realized that this approach wasn't right. I learned that when someone genuinely values you, you won't have to compromise your beliefs; they will actually complement and support them. Even though I was young, my dad's advice helped me understand that the best way to choose a partner is to find someone who truly appreciates you for who you are. It's a wonderful feeling. I didn't always follow my dad's advice when it came to choosing a mate, and I learned that the hard way. However, through my experiences, I recognized the importance of healthy relationships and the value they can bring to one's life.

Money also became a tricky issue as I started to realize its power and pull. In my neighborhood, many were trying to make quick money through dishonest means, such as selling drugs, robbing people, or participating in pyramid scheme businesses, scamming others, or participating in other illegal activities. One day, I was offered a chance to get involved in something clearly shady. I hesitated but remembered my dad's advice. That night, I talked about my dilemma with him. He could tell from my body language that I was upset. Although I usually felt comfortable talking to my dad, this time I was more afraid of my mom—she was tough as nails.

I finally decided to open up to my dad about the proposition I had been presented with. Surprisingly, he didn't scold me. Instead, he asked, "What matters more: a quick dollar or your reputation?" He emphasized that money could come and go, but my values and integrity were something I would carry for life. He told me, with a straight face, "The easy money route often leads to prison or an early grave." I respected my dad and valued his guidance. Instead of taking the easy, quick cash route, I chose to get my first job at Subway. I remember it clearly: I made about $110 a week working part-time.

In comparison, the guys I knew from my neighborhood who dealt drugs could make what I earned in a week in just five minutes. It didn't take long for me to realize that I had made the right choice. Many of my peers left the community one by one, either by going to prison or facing an early death. My dad always told me that my decisions should align with my goals and, more importantly, my values. Witnessing how the drug trade and other quick-money schemes negatively impacted my community strengthened my determination to seek opportunities that reflected who I was and what I believed in.

Leadership was another area where values were put to the test. As I took on roles in school clubs and sports teams, I saw firsthand how some leaders compromised their integrity for the sake of popularity or to please others. My dad encouraged me to lead by example. He taught me that authentic leadership involves making tough decisions that may not be popular but are ultimately correct. I remember a moment when I had to stand up against a decision that felt morally wrong, even if it meant alienating some teammates. Remembering my dad's words, I spoke out. It was intimidating, but I understood that the situation was bigger than me. As a result, two young men who were about to be cut from an AAU team I was on stayed on the team and were able to do something positive instead of being cut. Most team members didn't like them because they weren't as skilled, but I realized they still added value because they hustled and played hard. Most importantly, I didn't want to see them get into trouble or become discouraged and give up. As a team leader and captain, I spoke up to the coach and team because it was the right thing to do. These two young men remained on the team, and their contributions significantly contributed to our success that summer. As a team, we bonded and genuinely enjoyed each other's company. This act of courage, standing up for what's right, was a learning experience for me as a leader, showing the power of integrity in leadership and inspiring others to do the same.

Fast forward to today, and those same lessons still hold true. As a leader in my workplace, I sometimes observe so-called leaders conforming to the status quo simply because that's how things have always been done. However, I can't operate with that kind of mindset. The decisions I make as a leader are rooted in my core values and beliefs, and I'm fully aware that authentic leadership may involve personal sacrifice. If that means not being popular, missing out on a promotion, or even being ostracized, I'm okay with that, and I hope you can understand and empathize with this perspective. I will always stand up for what I believe in. I once heard a great motivational speaker mention that it is important to stand up for your beliefs; otherwise, you risk falling victim to anything, as you may be swayed by anything that comes your way. My teammates in high school would sometimes say, "You need to be a part of the team and do what we do." I would always respond by saying I don't mind doing what the group is doing as long as it's the right thing. My dad always reminded me that real men do not compromise their values. This aligns with a scripture from the Bible, specifically 1 Corinthians 16:13-14, ESV, "Be watchful, stand firm in the faith, act like men, be strong."

Throughout my journey, my Christian faith has served as the foundation for my values. There have been moments of uncertainty, times when I was tempted to follow the crowd rather than my convictions. In those times, my father was a steady reminder of the strength of faith and the principles of love and respect embedded in our beliefs. As a family, we often sought divine guidance through prayer, reinforcing the idea that my faith was a compass guiding me through life's challenges. This unwavering faith has not only given me a moral compass but also provided reassurance and confidence in my decisions, knowing principles of love and respect guide me.

Reflecting on those early years, I am keenly aware of how much my father influenced my character. His words, "Never compromise your values," were more than advice—they were a vow to live by. This lesson, which I have carried into adulthood, has served as my guiding light through life's challenges, preserving my integrity. I am truly thankful for those impactful conversations, for the moments that once seemed overwhelming, and for a father who exemplified the strength of standing firm. Our family motto, a simple yet powerful mantra, captures our unity: "Together we pray, together we stay; no matter what, we stand tall every day." This focus on the family's role in shaping character reminds us of the shared experiences and values that connect us all.

Lesson 4

VALUE THE COMBINATION

On a warm summer afternoon, July 4, 1992, the sun hung high in a cloudless sky, casting a golden light across our backyard. I was 10 years old, counting down the days until my 11th birthday. The sun blazed overhead, creating a comforting warmth that clung to my skin. I found myself sitting on the patio with my dad, who was wearing his familiar blue work jumpsuit, the one he always put on during home projects. He was busy tending to the fire for the barbecue we were hosting, with smoke rising in lazy waves and mingling with the mouthwatering aroma of seasoned chicken, steak, and ribs sizzling on the grill. It was a scene filled with warmth, joy, and anticipation—a perfect setting for a family gathering, a place where you always feel at home.

As I sat there, my little sister, who is about a year and a half younger than me, darted across the yard, her laughter breaking through the peaceful quiet of the day. She chased after the bubbles she had just blown, each delicate orb catching bits of sunlight as they floated into the blue sky. Watching her joy reminded me of simpler times, and for a moment, everything felt perfect. Suddenly, my dad turned to me, a hint of nostalgia clouding his brow. "Do you remember the last time you saw your grandmother?" he asked, his voice blending warmth and sadness that made my heart ache. I nodded, memories rushing back — holidays filled with her laughter and love. Grandma, my mom's mother, had passed away in October 1991 at the age of 65, leaving a void that seemed impossible to fill.

She meant everything to our family; her presence brightened every gathering. I remember her warm smile and how she quoted scripture as if it were deeply ingrained in her being. Grandma held her strong voice and stern look like a shield; no one dared to be disrespectful in her presence. We all knew Grandma didn't play games; she was the matriarch, leading her family with love and strength. I also thought of times when I visited her and that sterile scent of the hospital, where the beeping machines created an unsettling rhythm. Even though illness had taken a toll on her, I still held onto the positive energy I felt during our last visit to the hospital. Granny, with a slight smile, asked my dad to save her a plate of barbecue from his weekend grill sessions.

"Why did you bring up Grandma?" I asked my dad, a knot forming in my throat. "She passed away last year."

Dad looked at me with a seriousness I wasn't used to. "Did you really believe that the last time we were at the hospital would be the last time you'd see her alive?"

As I looked into his face, sadness welled up in my eyes, and I said, "No, sir. I thought she would come home, sit with us, and share one of her favorite scriptures." His gaze softened, empathy filling his face. He continued, "That's the thing about people, son. You'll meet many along the way, and each moment you share is a treasure that doesn't come with a guarantee for tomorrow."

His words settled deep in my heart like a weight, causing me to ponder their meaning. I realized that life can change suddenly, transforming joy into sorrow in an instant. He talked about valuing our loved ones while they're with us and how fast life can shift. "It's important to value everyone present today, especially at gatherings like this," he emphasized. I thought about how often I had gotten lost in my own world during past family get-togethers, believing there would always be another chance to connect. The truth is that each moment is fleeting, and once it's gone, it can never be truly replaced. This realization filled me with a sense of urgency and a deep appreciation for the present, serving as a poignant reminder to cherish every moment as if it were the last.

In my youthful innocence, I blurted out, "What if we have more parties in the future?" I desperately wanted to rationalize my distractions, and my voice sought reassurance with a hint of hope.

Dad smiled, a hint of amusement in his expression. "Maybe we will. However, remember that every person you meet and every laugh you share has its own unique magic. Each gathering is a special moment;

once it's gone, it can never truly be replicated." As he spoke, the significance of his words wrapped around me, igniting a deeper understanding of our shared moments. We were surrounded by friends and family, living, breathing, and laughing together in the warm embrace of life. I thought back to the little things, the inside jokes whispered over half-eaten plates, those late-night runs to the liquor store full of laughter, crazy stories about his childhood, or quiet moments spent reminiscing under the stars while sitting on the porch in the backyard.

The wind picked up, blowing a burst of bubbles into the air, pulling my sister's laughter back to the porch as she returned with her bubble solution. Together, we chased the floating spheres, giggling as they burst against our fingertips. In that moment, surrounded by the warmth of family, my heart filled with gratitude. I felt a deep appreciation for my dad, the lessons he shared, and the joy of being in the moment.

"Let's be thankful for this time together," I proposed, glancing at my dad and then at my sister. "Let's make sure we have fun." His eyes sparkled with approval. "That's what I'm talking about." Pops would go on to say, "Make memories, be present, and cherish the ones you love." Over time, I've come to realize that the value of connections deepens as you see and appreciate those around you more.

From that day forward, I made it a point to practice the lesson I had learned. Whether making a simple phone call to a friend or planning dinner with family, I committed to being fully present. I treasured every laugh, every shared story, and every quiet moment of comfortable silence. Life is a collection of moments, and their richness depends on the people we share them with. It's the relation-ships we nurture and the moments we create that give life its true meaning. I was determined to honor that, always remembering the importance of valuing and nurturing the relationships that enrich our lives.

As guests started to arrive, I greeted everyone warmly and with gratitude. I watched the sun slowly sink in the sky, casting long shadows across our yard. I felt deeply fortunate to have my dad beside me, sharing lessons that shaped my understanding of love, loss, and the profound connection between them. It wasn't just about enjoying the celebration that day; it was a realization that every person present had their own story, their own magic waiting to be shared. There was laughter, love, and the simple joy of chasing bubbles on a warm summer afternoon. As a family, we watched the neighborhood fireworks show, which some friends and family organized illegally, but that's a story for another day. Nonetheless, these were the moments I would carry with me forever, a testament to the beauty of being present in the lives of those I cherished.

I challenge you, starting now, to commit to valuing and appreciating the people God has placed in your life and to enjoy each moment. Even if you face disappointing times with them, push through those challenges and love them despite their mistakes. I'll close this lesson with a scripture. The Bible says about love in 1 Peter 4:8, NIV, "Above all, love each other deeply, because love covers over a multitude of sins."

Lesson 5

HOW TO WIN ANY WAR

When most people think of war, they typically envision the weapons and tactics required for victory. They picture maps spread out on tables, soldiers carefully positioned, and the sound of metal clinking as soldiers prepare for battle. It all feels immediate and real. Each conflict has its own unique strategies and tools, shaped by the complexities of its battlefield. However, one fall afternoon when I was 14 years old, I learned about a different kind of warfare from an unexpected source: Daddy Tyler.

I had just started high school at Lincoln High in the heart of South Dallas as a freshman. On the first day of football practice, I got into a fight with a young man I will call "Bonton" for the sake of this story. Bonton came up to me about something trivial—though I can't quite remember what it was—but I knew it was insignificant. While we were in the locker room, Bonton clenched his fist, got into a fighting stance, and said, "I'll beat your ass. Bitch ass nigga." I looked at him, quickly assessing the situation with tact and kept my distance.

To my surprise, one of our coaches heard the commotion and left the locker room at the worst possible moment. I personally think he knew it was about to go down. I had learned from previous experiences to take people's threats seriously. When the coach walked out of the locker room, I thought to myself, *'It's about to go down.'* So, I threw the first punch, and the fight was on. It didn't last long; I came out unscathed, helped him up, and that was the end of it.

Following the fight, we went to practice, and everything seemed to be over, but deep down, I knew this beef wasn't over. Bonton was a member of the notorious gang called the "Bloods," and based on my observations of how gang members operate, I was certain I would get jumped by multiple guys the next day.

When I got home, I was ready to share what had just happened at school with my dad. He was sitting in his La-Z-Boy, relaxing and watching the news. I sat on the couch facing him, and he noticed my body language—worried and scared. Before I could say anything, I heard him murmur softly to himself. Curious, I looked over; he had his eyes closed, seeming deep in concentration as if navigating an unseen battlefield. When I asked what he was doing, he opened his eyes and smiled, inviting me to join him.

"This," he said, gesturing with his hands in the air in what I interpreted as a posture of praise or worship, "is more powerful than any weapon." He placed a hand over his heart. "This is how we fight our battles."

"What do you mean?" I asked, intrigued but skeptical. I imagined knives, guns, and a strategic plan, anything but what he was suggesting.

He leaned back, letting out a small chuckle. "When I was your age, I thought war was all about strategy, numbers, and firepower. I studied the art of war; man, did you forget I fought in World War II? Son, I can tell you are going through something, but you will be okay." He continued, his voice carrying the weight of experience and wisdom, "But one day, during my own struggles, I learned something profound. Life isn't so different from war. We all have our battles, some small, some monumental. You'll face dilemmas, heartbreaks, and failures that seem insurmountable. But the most potent weapon you can wield isn't found on a battlefield; it's discovered in kneeling down in prayer." His words were like a beacon of light in the darkness, enlightening me in a way I had never encountered before.

I was completely taken aback. *Kneeling in prayer? How could that possibly help me confront the battles of life and the overwhelming challenges that filled me with anxiety?* What he didn't realize was that I was just one person, feeling as if I were about to face an army of 300 gang members the very next day. But my father, with his deep understanding of life's struggles, was there to guide me.

Seeing my hesitation, he elaborated. "When I pray, I make an appeal to something greater than myself. I invite God into my struggles, asking for strength and guidance. Think about it, son: God fights our battles in ways we can't. He reaches the heart, softens the hardest of minds, and reveals paths we can't see. Prayer is like a key that unlocks the door to perseverance and strength."

His words hung in the air as I contemplated them. "But what if things don't always change after you pray?" I pressed, a hint of rebellion creeping into my voice.

"Ah," he replied with a wise nod. "That's the tricky part. Sometimes, battles don't resolve as we wish. But prayer isn't just about the outcome; it's about the process. It equips you, molds you, and gives you the resilience to face whatever comes next. Victory isn't only defined by winning; it's also about growing stronger, even in loss."

When he mentioned "loss," I thought to myself, *I might just lose this fight*, but in the end, I hoped to live and be able to talk about it one day. It was obvious; my heart was filled with fear and doubt. At that point, I decided not to tell him and just give this prayer thing a try.

That night, with fear looming large over my heart, I got on my knees. I closed my eyes and said, "Dear God, give me the courage, clarity, and wisdom to face whatever comes next. I'm unsure about how to resolve this conflict with Bonton. Still, I have decided to trust you to look after me and make this situation right. In all these things, I pray in Jesus' name, amen."

The next day at school, I wore an old T-shirt, some old blue jeans, and black combat boots. If I got into a fight, I wouldn't ruin any of my new clothes. As I moved from class to class, the weight of uncertainty about what might happen grew stronger by the minute. But by the end of the school day, I ran into Bonton and about 20 of his fellow gang members while walking to my final class of the day. My heart started racing as they approached me. I mentally braced myself for a fight, but something strange happened; Bonton smiled at me and said, "What's up?" in a friendly manner before continuing his way. I looked at him and said, "What up?" with a guarded smile, trying to disguise my fear. As I turned the corner and was out of sight of the guys, I leaned over in relief, thinking, *What in the world just happened?* In this pivotal moment, the fear I had been building within myself clashed with the echoes of my father's wisdom and the peace that came from the prayer I had just prayed the night before.

As I gathered myself, I was still shocked and on guard, just in case they were waiting for another opportunity to attack. I went to practice that day, and a few days passed, and things continued as usual without any issues. I would see Bonton in the hallway, and he would speak and act as if everything was okay between us. The following Friday of that week, which was a couple of days after the initial fight, a few of my teammates and

I were sitting together at lunch when, to my surprise, guess who joined us? Yep, it was Bonton. He walked up to me, gave me some dap, and started talking as if we were the best of friends. It puzzled me for a moment, but I went along with the energy he was giving, which was positive and calm. As the days passed, we grew closer, developing a relationship based on cordiality and mutual respect.

Reflecting on this experience, my faith and trust in God grew significantly. I realized that many conflicts are not purely adversarial but can become opportunities for growth, connection, and understanding. Prayer proved to be more than just a plea for help; it became a source of clarity, giving me the courage to face adversity with a calm heart rather than a combative spirit. I understood that the power of prayer is enormous, and it's the most powerful tool I have in my list of spiritual weapons. Eventually, I told my dad what happened, and he simply smiled and said, "I knew this day would come. I want you to understand how to deal with battles in your life." My dad explained that every struggle, even the painful ones, can serve a purpose. Just as battles shape the course of history, personal conflicts shape our character and resilience.

As I grew older, I faced many challenges. One of the toughest was losing my dad on May 3, 1999, which was particularly devastating. However, I applied the lessons he taught me and managed to get through that difficult time. His wisdom, a guiding light in my life, helped me overcome many other obstacles, including college exams, broken friendships, career choices, and a failed marriage. Each experience brought its own unique challenges, but with my father's wisdom etched deep in my heart, I regularly found solace in prayer. It became my grounding force, a shield against self-doubt, fear, failure, haters, jealousy, and all the devices used by the devil.

Years later, as I stood in my own living room as a father, I realized the full weight of his teachings. Watching my own children face their challenges, I feel proud to share the lesson he has taught me. "Remember, winning isn't always about defeating an opponent," I've told them. "Often, it's about equipping ourselves with the right strategy, the right mindset, and always, a simple prayer." I lead by example with my family through daily prayer sessions. This practice has brought us closer and uplifted us spiritually.

Through each of life's dilemmas, I have learned that moments of connection and reaching out to something greater help me navigate any battle ahead. In every struggle lies the opportunity for growth, reminding us that our strongest weapon comes from within. Often, the most meaningful victories are those we find inside our hearts.

Concluding this chapter, I am compelled to share the scripture that has been my source of strength in times of battle. The passage from Ephesians 6:10-18 emphasizes the importance of spiritual strength and preparedness. Paul urges believers to be strong in the Lord and to wear the full armor of God to defend against evil challenges. This armor includes the belt of truth, which symbolizes honesty; the breastplate of righteousness for moral integrity; feet fitted with readiness to share the gospel; the shield of faith to protect against spiritual attacks; the helmet of salvation for assurance of eternal life; and the sword of the Spirit, which is God's word. Believers are also encouraged to pray continually for themselves and others, remaining alert to spiritual battles. I believe that if you start praying with expectation, which demonstrates your trust in God, He will show up and make a difference in your life. In Matthew 7:7-8, the message is quite simple and encouraging: if you reach out to God and ask for what you need, He will respond. If you're searching for answers or guidance, you will find it, and if you knock on the door of opportunity, it will open for you. It's a reminder that God is always listening and ready to help us when we genuinely seek Him. I find this scripture to be true, so step out in faith and let the Lord fight your battles. Remember, your most important weapon in spiritual warfare is prayer.

My dad not only empowered me to face life's challenges with courage but also gave me a toolbox of wisdom to handle the complexities of human relationships. This lesson is a vital part of a strong foundation; it instills a sense of purpose and equips me with the tools to confront future struggles with faith, empathy, and understanding. Thus, the legacy of wisdom continues, instilling purpose and resilience across generations.

Interlude

Let's pause for a quick moment of reflection as we transition from dad's lessons to mom's lessons. As we shift our focus, let's take a moment to reflect on the unique perspectives each parent brought to my life.

The first half of this book shared lessons I learned from my dad. These lessons, like how to succeed in any challenge, the importance of valuing each moment with family, friends, and loved ones, and the significance of never compromising our values, are not just theoretical. They are practical tools designed to help you and give you confidence to navigate life, no matter what stage you're in—whether you're a teenager, a young adult, middle-aged, or older.

The second half of the book is a journey of empowerment, focusing on the lessons I learned from my mom. She was straightforward and unfiltered. Momma Tyler did not sugarcoat anything; her approach was more direct, unlike the subtler tactics my dad used. This next section of the book provides snapshots of five lessons I learned from my mom—lessons that can be applied across various areas of our lives, empowering us to take charge of our own destinies.

Lessons From Momma Tyler

Lesson 6

THE POWER OF FAITH

I can't talk about faith without mentioning my mom, Ann Tyler, whom I affectionately call "Momma Tyler." She was the heartbeat of our family, a beacon of hope even in the toughest times. Growing up, we didn't have much, and money was often tight, but our faith was strong. Momma Tyler would walk around our home and pray over it, claiming things as if they were already done. Seeing my mom pray the way she did instilled a strong sense of faith in our family. One of her most powerful methods was incorporating prayer into our daily lives. At mealtimes, the family would join hands and give thanks, acknowledging God's blessings despite financial struggles. In the evenings, especially during challenging times, our family would gather in the living room to pray together. We would share our hopes and dreams while also supporting one another through difficulties. We could feel God's presence among us, creating a powerful connection during our prayers. Afterwards, I experienced a comforting sense of peace. Matthew 18:20 highlights the presence of Jesus when people come together in His name, emphasizing that God is with us in moments of fellowship and unity. This verse reminds us of the strength and support found in togetherness and shared faith. Those times of coming together and praying were limitless, shaping and guiding me in ways I didn't fully understand until a pivotal Christmas season when I was just nine years old. I mentioned earlier that I wanted a Nintendo, but it was too expensive. Well, in this chapter, you will learn what the hype was all about surrounding this Nintendo experience.

On a busy Saturday morning at Walmart, the store was off the chain with families gathering supplies for the upcoming holidays. As I navigated through the crowded aisles filled with cheerful shoppers, something caught my eye. There, shining under the bright fluorescent lights, was a table displaying a brand-new Nintendo system, decorated with a bright red bow. My heart lifted; it was exactly what I had dreamed of for Christmas.

Excitement bubbled over as I rushed to my mom, tugging at her sleeve. "Look, Mom! I want this for Christmas!" My heart raced as she followed me to the table. But when she glanced at the price tag, my heart sank. $199—a staggering amount for us. I braced myself for the inevitable "no," but my mom's reaction took me by surprise.

With a twinkle in her eye and a warm smile, she said, "Baby, look! There's a drawing for this game! I'm going to win it for you in Jesus' name!" Her confidence was contagious. I watched her as she filled out the entry form, determination shining brightly within her. "You have to have faith and believe, and you shall receive," she said, gently squeezing my shoulder. Her words were a reminder of the power of prayer, as we were taught in Matthew 21:22. This scripture emphasizes that when you pray with genuine belief, you can receive whatever you ask for. It emphasizes the significance of faith in the transformative power of prayer. This verse was a source of strength and hope for us.

Despite my mom's inspiring words, doubt started to creep in as I watched the long line of other hopeful kids and their parents. I felt hopelessly outmatched. Still, my mom's unwavering smile was a powerful thing, and at that moment, I shared her belief, if only for a little while.

Days passed, and the anticipation of Christmas grew heavier in the air. I tucked the memory of that Nintendo away, but doubt seeped back in each day. Christmas Eve arrived, and as I lay in bed, I surrounded myself with the simple joys I had learned to cherish. We baked cookies, shared stories, sang carols, and simply enjoyed each other's company. Christmas Eve was always magical, filled with love and laughter, and this year was no different, despite the gaming system remaining a distant dream.

As the clock ticked closer to midnight, I drifted into sleep, blissfully unaware of the surprise waiting to unfold. Christmas morning arrived with lively laughter and the smell of a delicious breakfast filling our home. As we gathered around the tree, my heart raced at the sight of small gifts. My mom handed out the presents while my little sister bounced around happily.

And then, I saw it—a large box wrapped in shimmering paper, tied with the familiar red bow I had admired at Walmart. My heart stopped. I bolted across the room, tearing the paper as if my life depended on it. There it was, a brand-new Nintendo system, exactly what I had wished for! I was in shock. My mom beamed, "See, Baby? You had faith, and God delivered!" Her joy and pride in that moment were palpable, serving as a testament to the power of faith, not just in individual lives, but in strengthening relationships and building a supportive family.

In that moment, I truly saw what faith looks like. It wasn't just about believing in something big; it was about the heart and conviction behind it. My mom's steadfast belief turned hope into reality, showing that miracles often come to those who dare to believe. This experience taught me that faith is not only a belief but also a powerful force that can turn dreams into reality if we hold onto it with unwavering conviction.

I couldn't wait to use this new super-power called faith. When school resumed after the holiday break, my fourth-grade teacher, Ms. Cannon, held weekly drawings for students who had behaved well. The chance to win prizes like water guns, yo-yos, board games, and tasty snacks fueled my imagination. I decided to approach the drawing just as my mom had taught me.

With the same fervor my mother exhibited, I filled my heart with faith. I told my classmates and Ms. Cannon that I would win before the drawing took place. The week went by, and lo and behold, my name was the first one pulled! I couldn't contain my joy, shouting with excitement. This faith thing was real, and it brought me so much joy and excitement! It was a moment of shared faith and celebration within our community, reflecting the unity and support we find in 1 Thessalonians 5:11, NIV, which states, "Therefore encourage one another and build each other up, just as in fact you are doing."

After school, I rushed home and shared my experience with my mom. She listened, a proud smile illuminating her face. As she flipped through her Bible, she shared Hebrews 11:1, NKJV, "Now faith is the substance of things hoped for, the evidence of things not seen." She explained that this principle was exactly what I had practiced.

Over the next two weeks, I applied the same principle. Each week, my name was drawn repeatedly. At one point, my faith grew so strong that Ms. Cannon had to change the rules because I kept winning. It was a testament to the power of faith, leaving me feeling accomplished and empowered. Faith has been the foundation of how I handle life's challenges and experiences. My mom taught me that faith is a powerful force, capable of moving mountains, delivering Christmas miracles, and creating unforgettable moments for a nine-year-old. With faith, dreams transform from distant fantasies into achievable realities, reminding me that belief can light the darkest paths. I know that I wouldn't be where I am today without faith.

However, I must emphasize that faith alone is not the key to my success. It also requires effort, taking initiative, and doing the work. Every goal I have accomplished and every milestone I have reached were achieved through a combination of hard work and faith. The passage from James 2:14-17 inspires us to recognize that faith without action is ineffective. It prompts a reflection on how genuine faith should naturally lead to good works in serving those in need, such as providing food and clothing to the less fortunate. Merely expressing faith or offering well-wishes, without taking concrete steps to help others, makes such faith meaningless. Ultimately, it reminds us that true faith shines through our actions.

My mom used to always tell me to put my trust completely in God. After hearing her speak so often about trusting God, I asked her, if you can trust God without faith? I know this may sound like a dumb question, but I wanted to hear her response. She replied, "No, you can't trust God without faith. Baby, you have all the faith you need; just know that. Your trust and your faith go hand in hand." I encourage you to embrace the power of faith in all areas of your life, and I have faith you will experience the power of God in your life.

Lesson 7

SEED TIME AND HARVEST TIME

Momma Tyler was the most generous person I have ever known. Her heart seemed limitless, always willing to share what little we had with those around us. It was common for her to give clothes to friends or strangers, food to neighbors, and large sums of money to the church. She also often helped family and friends in need.

Momma Tyler's unwavering belief in generosity came from several pivotal events in her life. I remember my mom sharing her childhood experiences growing up in a household that faced the challenges of scarcity. Despite the struggles, the warmth that came from acts of generosity during tough times left a lasting impression on her. There were times when her family faced significant difficulties, and they would receive unexpected blessings from the Lord. Kind neighbors occasionally brought them food and clothes when they had very little. These acts of kindness had a profound impact on her, shaping her belief that helping others can lighten their burdens and inspire a spirit of giving.

Throughout her life, Momma Tyler faced many challenges, losses, illnesses, and financial struggles that only reinforced her understanding of the power of generosity. She often shared stories of how, during her darkest times, help came from unexpected places. Whether it was a friend stopping by with a meal or someone offering help during tough moments, these experiences taught her that giving not only lifts others but also builds a support network that often comes back to you. These hardships, including the death of her husband, my dad, and her own health problems, were tough, but they never stopped her from her mission of giving.

As a child, I struggled to understand the concept of generosity, especially when my mom gave away money that I felt we couldn't afford to part with.

Momma Tyler had a special talent for making strangers feel like family. On any given day, our home could be full of visitors, as friends stopped by to engage in lively conversations, often jokingly referred to as gossip. Neighbors would share a cup of tea, and even those we hardly knew might come by looking for a warm meal or a kind word. My mom was always eager to talk about the goodness of God. No one left her home empty-handed; she would send them off with baked goods, clothes she found at Goodwill, or even new items she never wore, along with a few dollars she could barely spare.

Every time she emptied her pockets, it felt like part of our limited resources also disappeared. Still, she carried her generosity like a badge of honor. People received not only material items but also Bible scriptures, leaving them feeling inspired and uplifted in her presence.

When I was young, about 11 or 12 years old, I didn't understand why she gave so much. Naturally, as a kid who didn't have much, I didn't realize the true benefits and freedom that come with giving. My mom always said that it's better to give than to receive, a concept that seemed wrong to me at the time. I recall feeling a mix of confusion, frustration, and even a hint of resentment towards my mom's generosity.

One particularly chilly winter afternoon, my cousin Diane came over and needed a place to stay. My mom welcomed her in with open arms. At that time, Diane was still in high school, and my mom had taken her in as if she were her own. I don't remember the details of how she ended up at our house or the back-and-forth conversations between Diane's mom, my aunt Mary, and my mom. Still, I recall thinking that we barely had enough resources for our immediate family.

That night, I witnessed the transformative power of my mom's generosity. I watched my mom comfort Diane, her warmth shining brightly against the cold world outside, turning our cramped living room into a haven. The laughter and conversation soon filled the air, and I couldn't help but feel a shift within myself. Diane's frown turned into a gentle smile. At that moment, I realized that sometimes love and support can outweigh even the most uncomfortable circumstances, providing reassurance and security to those in need.

It was a moment of deep relief, a reassurance that we would be okay, and a realization that our family had grown to include one more person. Our home became a safe haven of kindness, filled with laughter and conversations, where people found solace, peace, and support. Our house became home to many, a testament to the lasting impact of Momma Tyler's generosity.

However, that night before I went to bed, I couldn't shake the image from my mind. "Why do you give away so much?" I asked my mom, my curiosity mingling with a hint of frustration. "It's just the right thing to do," she replied, her eyes sparkling with a light that seemed to come from her very soul. "When we share what we have, we're planting seeds. It may not feel like much now, but one day, those seeds will bear fruit in ways we least expect." She was referring to the idea that acts of kindness and generosity, like seeds, have the potential to grow and multiply, often in ways we cannot foresee.

I struggled to understand her words; to me, it seemed that every time she gave, we lost a little more of what we had. "But we're not rich, Mom! What if we don't have enough for ourselves?" I asked.

My mom's response to my question was a lesson. She looked at me, her eyes filled with a light that shone from her very soul, and said, "Sweetheart, what I'm offering is not just about money or items. It's about love, kindness, and faith. When you give from your heart, you create a cycle of generosity. Sometimes, you'll find that what you've sown returns to you in unexpected ways." This lesson stayed with me for the rest of my life, teaching me the value of kindness and faith, and uplifting my spirit with its profound wisdom.

As the years passed, the seeds of generosity my mom had planted began to produce unexpected results. We often received help when we needed it most, such as surprise checks and random gifts from people my mom had helped before. The warmth and love we shared came back around, strengthening our belief in the cycle of generosity and inspiring hope in the unexpected ways it returns.

I remember a particularly challenging time when our only mode of transportation broke down and bills started to pile up. Just as we thought we might give up, a mechanic we knew told my mom that it was on his heart to fix the car for free. This was the same person to whom my mom would randomly deliver home-cooked meals at the shop to show appreciation for taking such good care of our family vehicle.

Once our family vehicle reached the end of its life and became too old and problematic to repair, we received an unexpected check that was large enough to buy a brand-new Cadillac. My mom looked at my siblings and me and yelled, "Harvest time!" She was referring to the biblical idea of reaping what you sow, a testament to the fact that our acts of generosity often come back to us in surprising ways. This cycle of giving and receiving continued throughout my childhood and teenage years, reassuring us that generosity always comes back in unexpected ways.

As I grew older, I began to understand the deep wisdom behind my mom's constant generosity. Momma Tyler taught me that generosity isn't about how much you have, but about your willingness to share what you can. It's about connection and compassion that truly count. She always believed the Lord would take care of us. Years later, I found myself in the world, carrying on the legacy of kindness that Momma Tyler had instilled in me. I realized that generosity isn't measured by wealth but by the openness of your heart. Just as God cares for the birds and flowers, He would take care of all of us. Reflecting on Matthew 6, I remembered her words and how they connected with the scripture. I learned through experience that seeking God first and His kingdom should reflect in how we treat each other. As a result, we won't have to worry about anything because the good Lord will not fail to meet our needs.

The life lessons hidden in all those moments of giving in some shape, form, or fashion began to unveil themselves slowly, and I started to understand that Momma Tyler wasn't just nurturing relationships; she was cultivating a garden of generosity that blossomed far beyond our front yard.

As I ventured into the world, I carried with me the lessons of kindness, compassion, and the belief that true wealth is found not in material possessions but in the bonds we forge with others. Momma Tyler taught me that every act of giving, no matter how small, can spark a ripple effect of love that illuminates our paths, reminding us that we are part of something much larger, a family built on shared hearts and open hands.

Reflecting on my childhood and upbringing, I see how Momma Tyler's gifts extended beyond material items; they created bonds that connected many people. She taught me the importance of both giving and receiving. Her spirit lives on in me as I continue to plant seeds of generosity, knowing that the harvest time will come, not measured by the abundance of possessions but by the wealth of relationships, love, and care we cultivate together.

I witnessed how Mom's kindness often returned to our family in unexpected ways, fostering a belief in the cycle of generosity. We learned to view challenges not as obstacles but as opportunities to practice the same compassion we had seen her embody. As we interact with our families, we have adopted similar values, leading our own lives with an emphasis on giving back, helping others, and nurturing community connections, just as Momma Tyler did.

Ultimately, Momma Tyler's legacy of generosity not only enriched her life and the lives of those around her but also instilled a lifelong commitment to kindness in everyone she encountered. I became an ambassador for her ideals, proving that the seeds of generosity she had planted flourished well beyond our own families, creating a ripple effect that continued to spread and inspire for generations to come.

I encourage you to seize every opportunity to give, as you will undoubtedly feel the power of giving. Remember that generosity comes in various forms. It could be as simple as a sincere smile, a random visit to a nursing home, or even buying someone's groceries. Each small gesture has the potential to make a positive difference in someone's life. There's no doubt that your harvest time will always be timely and plentiful.

Lesson 8

DON'T MISS A SPOT

Growing up in the Tyler household, one rule stood out above all others: "Don't miss a spot." Momma Tyler, our fierce matriarch, enforced this mantra like a true drill sergeant. From the moment I woke up, the air was thick with the scent of Pine-Sol and the almost musical sounds of her scrub brush sweeping across the kitchen floor. As a kid, I didn't see chores as responsibilities; I saw them as hurdles I had to clear to avoid my mother's wrath. Momma Tyler's strict standards for cleanliness came from her own upbringing and experiences that shaped her perspective on discipline and respect for one's environment. Growing up in a household where everyone had a role in keeping things in order, she believed that cleanliness wasn't just a chore but a fundamental way to show respect for yourself and your home. Her own mother had enforced similar standards, often reminding her of the value of hard work and the pride that comes from doing a job well. The chaos of a messy home reminded her of her past struggles, and she was determined to instill a sense of order in her children's lives to prevent them from facing the same chaos.

At seven years old, I stood in the living room, about to go into the kitchen. The sight that met me was intimidating—pots scattered across the stove, plates spread out on the bar, and a sink full of dishes. The idea of dealing with this mess on my own was frightening. The heavy feeling of responsibility and the fear of not meeting Momma Tyler's standards weighed on me.

I clutched a rag in my small hands while Momma Tyler stood over me, scrutinizing my every move. "If you miss a spot," she warned, her voice sharp and piercing. She nodded at me and said firmly, "Get it done or else." At that moment, it felt as if my mom were seven feet tall. I knew she meant business, and the unspoken threat hung in the air like a dark cloud. We all understood what that meant: a dreaded "whooping" awaited anyone who fell short of her high standards.

Despite the pressure, I managed to finish the task. I don't know exactly how long it took, but it was over three hours. By the time I was done, every bone in my body ached.

Saturday mornings were especially intense in our house. Each room was assigned to a different family member. I often found myself stuck with the bathrooms, a role that was both dreaded and respected. Armed with disinfectant and a toothbrush for scrubbing the grout, I cleaned with a level of fervor that belied my age. But I was not alone in this. I learned to delegate tasks and depend on others to reach a common goal. Although chores were often met with resistance and complaints, those times became moments for teamwork and camaraderie. Over time, the shared experience of tackling household chores fostered a sense of mutual respect among my family. We learned to appreciate each other's strengths and weaknesses, as some excelled at cleaning while others might have been better at assembling things. This dynamic helped build a bond that would last beyond childhood, teaching us to support each other in all aspects of life.

On one unusually chilly Saturday morning, I focused on the tiny tiles that lined our bathroom floor, which had collected grime like a badge of honor. I scrubbed tirelessly, hypnotized by the steady sound of bristles against porcelain. But as I worked, I felt my fingers start to ache, and a creeping doubt wormed its way into my mind. I paused and looked at my reflection in the mirror, just a kid determined to conquer this stubborn dirt. "Don't miss a spot," I told myself, pouring every ounce of energy into my scrubbing. The fear of punishment if I didn't meet Momma Tyler's standards weighed heavily on my shoulders, pushing me to do my best. I remembered the first time she praised my work when I left the bathroom shining like new. That brief moment of approval motivated me more than anything else. I wanted to earn that praise again.

Stepping back to admire my work, I felt a wave of satisfaction washing over me. I did it. The tiles gleamed under the lights, each one a testament to my effort. I couldn't wait to show Momma Tyler.

Freedom hovered over me, and for a moment, I savored the triumph of finishing

a task well. But then reality set in. I remembered her usual routine of inspecting every
corner of our house. With my heartbeat
quickening, I waited for her to come into
the bathroom, her sharp eyes sweeping over
the floor. She paused, and for a moment, I
thought I saw a glimmer of approval in her
eyes. "Not bad," she said, but then her brow
furrowed. "Did you get behind the toilet?"
My heart sank. I had indeed forgotten that
little spot, often called no-man's land. She
knelt, and I immediately felt discouraged.
"Come here," she commanded. I stepped forward, bracing myself for the consequences.
Instead of an explosion of anger, however,
she sighed deeply, her voice softening. "Do
you see this?" She pointed to the dirt that
stubbornly clung to the shadows. "Every spot
matters, not just in cleaning, but in life, too."
She looked at me with a stern expression,
and I thought to myself, *Oh no, I'm about to
get a beating*. Instead, she quoted Colossians

3:17 from the Bible, which I paraphrase: "Whatever you do, do it in the name of Jesus and give Him the glory for everything." Her words echoed in my mind, shaping my understanding of diligence and pride in all aspects of life. This experience taught me that every task, no matter how small, deserves our full attention and effort, and that's a lesson I carry with me to this day.

Standing there, I absorbed the weight of her words. The consequences of my actions went far beyond just a "whooping;" they shaped my character, teaching me the importance of hard work and taking pride in everything I did. It wasn't just about avoiding punishment; it was about learning to care, nurture, and ensure that whatever I undertook was done with purpose and respect.

The mantra "don't miss a spot" became a guiding principle, instilling a sense of diligence and pride in every task undertaken. Whether it was maintaining a job, completing schoolwork, or engaging with others in developing a community event, I approached each responsibility with the mindset that attention to detail mattered. This approach not only led to personal achievements, such as promotions and respect from peers, but also fostered a sense of integrity that defined my character. The lessons learned from those early chores transformed into resilience and a proactive attitude, and I am committed to excellence in everything I do.

This lesson was transformative, and it would guide my actions and decisions in the years to come. It was a reassuring presence, a constant reminder of the importance of diligence and pride in all my endeavors. This guiding principle can provide reassurance and direction to anyone on their own journey of personal growth and development.

This lesson followed me into adulthood. At 20 years old, I was blessed to secure a job at a well-known burger joint while attending Texas Southern University in Houston, Texas. I was grateful for the opportunity to work. Initially, my primary responsibilities included keeping the lobby clean, cleaning the bathrooms, and ensuring the entry doors and windows were spotless. If you've been following along, you might guess what was going through my mind while I cleaned: "Don't miss a spot."

I scrubbed those floors as if my life depended on it, ensuring the lobby looked and smelled like a five-star establishment. I treated each customer like family, making an effort to learn their names while they dined with us. I went the extra mile by offering refills, and sometimes, when they wanted to order additional food, I would take their orders at their tables. Although this was unorthodox, I always remembered to serve others as if I were doing work for the Lord.

After three weeks of working at this spot, I was offered a shift manager position.

There was no doubt that the lesson I learned on that Saturday morning earned me a pay raise, but it also helped me gain the respect of the customers and my coworkers. That said, through my experience, I have learned that sometimes you may not receive the respect you deserve from the people you serve or from some of your coworkers. Still, I always knew that doing things the right way was bigger than me, and not missing a spot was ingrained in my spirit.

The lesson of not missing the spot resonated with me on many levels. Years later, as I scrub my own home or take on a tough project, I remember Momma Tyler's words and the importance of those lessons. While I may no longer fear the sting of her belt, I carry her teachings with me. The grit of those early Saturday mornings shaped my character, instilling a sense of pride in my work and life. Today, I realize that whether a space is clean or messy, it's not the environment that truly matters; it's how you choose to respect it that lasts a lifetime.

Overall, the combination of a structured upbringing, the bond my siblings and I built through our shared responsibilities, and the lasting effect of those early lessons created a strong foundation for us. It not only shaped our views on work and responsibility but also served as a lasting source of motivation, guiding us through life's ups and downs.

This lesson has not only served me well in terms of having character and integrity in my work, but also in understanding that when you value what you have, your territory grows. The Lord will bless you with more and more as you learn to value and appreciate what you possess. Please take this lesson to heart and apply it to everything you do, ensuring that you don't miss a spot.

Lesson 9

IMPLEMENTATION THROUGH IMAGINATION

In a neighborhood where dreams often faded under the weight of harsh realities, within these vibrant streets of the Southeast side of Dallas, Texas (Pleasant Grove), society painted a limited picture of what your future looked like as a Black kid. Growing up, my teachers or adult family members would ask me and my friends, "What do you want to be when you become an adult?" It's interesting how our responses were often shaped by the society we lived in: schoolteacher, business owner, pro athlete, rapper, actor, and, jokingly, some would say, a pimp or a hustler. At only nine years old, I aspired for what felt far beyond my reach, bolstered solely by the encouraging words of Momma Tyler.

Momma Tyler was a powerhouse in many ways. With her impeccable sense of style, she transformed ordinary moments into something special. Though our financial struggles were evident, she always looked stunningly wealthy. Her full-length mink coat moved through the chilly air like a flowing river, and every Sunday, she dressed my siblings and me in suits and dresses that would make any family proud. Everyone in the neighborhood thought we were a wealthy family, amazed by her seemingly effortless grace despite the hardships she faced.

One day, after a Sunday service full of optimism, Momma Tyler called me into the dimly lit living room, where a full-length mirror stood proudly against the wall. She motioned for me to join her. I remember my mom looking in the mirror and saying with great confidence that she was rich and beautiful. "Look at this mirror, Mavin," she said, her voice steady with conviction. "What do you see?"

I hesitated, my cheeks warming with uncertainty. My speech impediment made its presence known as I hesitantly mumbled, "I-I'm Mavin, I'm from the hood, and I want to go to c-college one day." Each word was a mountain to climb, stuttered and faltered, each pause dripping with insecurity.

Momma Tyler's radiant smile reflected back at me, and she said, "Do you believe that? Did you see the greatness in what you just said?" "M-maybe," I replied, my little heart pounding in my chest. "You must visualize it, Mavin! You have to see it before you can ever achieve it." Her reflection blended with mine as she leaned closer. "Imagine yourself in that cap and gown, celebrating with the family, ready to take on the world." As I recall this moment, tears well up in my eyes. It was the first time I truly believed that being somebody special was within my reach. For that fleeting moment, I saw myself in that cap and gown, ready to conquer the world with fervor and enthusiasm.

Following Momma Tyler's advice, I started visualizing my future every day. Standing in front of that mirror, I would affirm, "I am Mavin. I am a great speaker. I will attend college." With each repetition, my stutter became softer, and my confidence grew stronger. Visualization became a powerful tool in my personal growth journey, filling me with a sense of empowerment and confidence. This practice, grounded in faith and determination, not only transformed my self-image but also paved the way for my future success, inspiring me to chase my dreams and showing the transformative power of visualization.

At school, my confidence increased, and gradually, the walls of fear started to fall. I began participating in church plays and even taking on leadership roles at school and with my sports teams. Every accomplishment, no matter how small, was fueled by that daily positive glance in the mirror.

As high school graduation was nearing, my dreams began to become reality. I had worked hard, visualized strongly, and brought those visions to life through countless hours of effort. It was time to walk across that stage in a cap and gown, and it hit me: I was living out my childhood dream.

The day was bright, and the crowd erupted in cheers as my name echoed across the sanctuary. In my last year of high school, I attended and graduated from a small Christian school. Momma Tyler, dressed in her finest attire, stood proudly in the front row, tears shining in her eyes. I spotted her and understood that this moment wasn't just my triumph but a testament to the power of imagination ignited by nurturing belief. It was a bittersweet moment. I graduated and achieved a great goal, but my dad had passed away a few days before my graduation. I graduated as salutatorian of my class and was accepted into Wiley College in Marshall, Texas, where I began my higher education journey. However, not having my dad at my graduation was a tough moment for me. I remembered his teachings and clung to the lessons he and my mom had shared with me, as if my life depended on it. I went off to college the following fall and didn't look back. Momma Tyler's unwavering belief in me, her nurturing influence, was a guiding light in my journey, showing me the power of positive influence in shaping one's destiny. It made me feel supported and guided and inspired me to be that guiding light for others.

Later, after my graduation, when I got home, I saw that mirror once again. "I am Mavin," I grinned, looking at the reflection that now radiated a belief once absent.

During my time in college, I faced several specific challenges that tested my resolve and determination. One of the main hurdles was managing the academic demands of college coursework, which proved to be much more challenging than high school, while also trying to stay financially afloat. I was completely broke. I often struggled with feelings of inadequacy, especially when surrounded by peers who seemed more prepared or confident. My early struggles with a speech impediment resurfaced in classroom settings, making participation intimidating at times and shaking the confidence I had worked hard to build through visualization and affirmation. But I held onto my faith and determination, knowing that these challenges were just stepping stones on my path to success, and that with faith and perseverance, any obstacle can be overcome, enabling me to face and conquer them.

Amid challenges, my relationship with Momma Tyler changed deeply. Each call became a source of support. I not only looked for her guidance but also felt more responsible for carrying on the legacy of strength she had given me. When she shared stories of her sacrifices and dreams, I saw how closely our paths were connected. My successes were not just mine; they reflected her struggles and victories. As I continued to move forward, I became increasingly involved in campus activities, joined the prestigious Black fraternity of the Divine 9, Phi Beta Sigma Inc., and participated in events celebrating our culture. During these times, I learned the power of community and the importance of giving back. My father's voice echoed in my mind, reminding me, "Always look to uplift others."

Fueled by this principle, I organized tutoring sessions for students who struggled in their classes, choosing to share the resources I wish I had. Not only was I solidifying my own understanding, but I was also building a community where those in similar situations felt seen and valued. Graduation day arrived too quickly. As I put on another cap and gown, I felt the love and warmth of Momma Tyler wrapping around me, just like that full-length mink coat she wore so proudly. When I marched across the stage, a wave of emotion washed over me. It wasn't just about celebrating my achievements; I was honoring the sacrifices made by those who came before me. I'm referring to the resilient people who fought for our educational rights during the civil rights movement, as well as my parents, whose teachings, woven into my fabric, gave me strength. After graduation, the world was wide open. With a degree in hand and a heart full of dreams, I stood in front of that same mirror I'd grown up with. It was a symbol of my journey and a constant reminder of the power of imagination and resilience. As I looked at my reflection, I knew I was ready to take on the world, not only for myself but for the community I come from. My journey was just beginning, but the impact of my father's teachings and Momma Tyler's belief changed my life. Now, it's my turn to inspire the next generation—to help them see their own greatness and potential. Where dreams once faded in the shadows of my neighborhood, I stand as a beacon of hope, echoing my parents' wisdom: "You are the master of your destiny." The legacy of resilience, love, and unwavering faith will continue—not just in my life, but in the lives of those I influence, instilling in them the same resilience that has guided me.

The cycle of imagination and action didn't stop after I achieved my goals of graduating from high school, college, and overcoming my stutter. However, I still apply the principle of Imagination and Implementation today. The grind never stops, and how we see ourselves reflects who we are and what we become. After reading the book *Grow Rich* by Napoleon Hill, my main takeaway is that we have the power to shape our own lives and environments. It is our personal responsibility to do so, and we have the ability to influence our own destiny. You can influence, direct, and control your own environment. You can make your life what you want it to be." My mom, who's never read this book, somehow understood this principle. I saw firsthand how powerful it is to imagine and visualize yourself doing exactly what you desire, and to act as if you are exactly what you believe you are. For example, when she wanted to start her own clothing business, she would spend hours visualizing herself as a successful entrepreneur and acting as if she were already running her business. Lo and behold, one day I looked up and saw her selling clothes and running a successful business. Regardless of the circumstances, we can rise above any predicament. Let me clarify: although my mom did not read the book *Think and Grow Rich*, she understood the word of God very well. Many of the principles I was raised on came directly from the Word of God. Momma Tyler was an avid reader, but her primary source for applying values in our home came from the Word of God, which gave us strength and hope on our journey. This understanding of the power of self-image and faith-based principles empowers us to take control of our destiny and rise above any circumstance.

Regardless of the environment you're in, even in the toughest circumstances where dreams struggle to take flight, I discovered the most profound secret of all: every journey begins with the image of who we dare to become. Proverbs 23:7 expresses the importance of our thoughts. This scripture emphasizes that a person's thoughts shape their character and identity. Essentially, it suggests that our mindset and beliefs influence who we are and how we act. This principle meant everything to my mom. I learned from this lesson that how you see yourself is a true indicator of who you may become. In that realization, I became a beacon of hope, embodying Momma Tyler's unwavering belief that action starts with imagination and that our self-image is the key to unlocking our potential for personal growth.

Lesson 10

WELL DONE, GOOD AND FAITHFUL SERVANT

Being around Momma Tyler was like a rollercoaster ride. We went through many ups and downs, but I learned a lot from her along the way. My time with Momma Tyler was filled with a whirlwind of experiences. We faced our share of highs and lows, but I always knew she had my back.

I learned invaluable lessons from her. She taught me the importance of being faithful with the blessings God has given me, living a life that is pleasing to the Lord, and not giving up during tough times. She emphasized the importance of leaving a powerful legacy and making sure I provide an inheritance for the next generation. Most importantly, she showed me that I should place my faith and trust not in people or the government, but in the Lord.

Momma Tyler instilled in me the ultimate goal of hearing the Lord say, "Well done, good and faithful servant," a phrase that signifies the highest form of praise in the Christian faith.

From my earliest memories, Momma Tyler was a force of nature. Her laughter, a symphony of joy, filled our modest home like a gospel concert, weaving happiness into the fabric of my childhood. Each note of her joyful laugh danced through the air, replaying in my mind during the most cherished moments of my life. She was not just a source of joy but also a pillar of strength, standing firm during the inevitable storms that came our way.

Life wasn't always easy for us. I remember the struggles, the heartaches, and the times when hope felt like a distant dream. Yet through every dark cloud, Momma held her chin high, with unwavering faith that could move mountains. Her faith, a cornerstone of her resilience, became the very foundation upon which I built my understanding of overcoming adversity, serving as a beacon of hope in the darkest times.

One rainy afternoon, when I was about 23 years old, I felt compelled to visit her. I had just finished my probation as a new police officer and was brimming with excitement to share this milestone. It was just her and me. I remember the smell of rain mixing with the scent of her homemade chili as I entered her cozy home. I sat on a bar stool in the kitchen, my heart pounding in anticipation of her words of pride and encouragement. Meanwhile, she sat in the living room, her wise eyes locked on me even as thunder rolled in the distance.

Before I could speak, she leaned back and looked at me with a serious, focused gaze—one that made her wisdom feel deeply penetrating. "Child," she began, "life is going to throw curveballs at you. Always be faithful in the little things God has blessed you with. Treasure them, for they prepare you for greater gifts ahead." Her words sank into my heart, changing my outlook on life's challenges and blessings.

As I gazed out the window, watching raindrops race down the panes, I reflected on the challenges I had faced so far and the small blessings I had received from the good Lord. I had escaped an evil drug epidemic that trapped many in our community, a crisis that tested my faith in ways words can't express. I overcame my stutter and bore the loss of my father when I was just 17. My journey was full of trials, yet at that moment, I realized how those challenges had shaped me. I understood the importance of taking care of the little things I had and valuing everything I had been entrusted with. Every struggle was, indeed, an opportunity for growth and gratitude.

After sharing her words of wisdom, I told her I had completed probation. She smiled so broadly that it made me feel like the best officer who had ever worn a uniform. Although she was excited for me, she was quick to remind me that I am still a servant of the Lord and that I should police my community with fairness and compassion for the people I serve.

She frequently emphasized the importance of living a life that reflects God's love and grace. "In everything you do," she'd say, "it's not about perfection; it's about intention." This mantra became a guiding light, encouraging me to find ways to spread kindness, no matter how small, creating ripples of change around me. Her words still inspire me today, a testament to the lasting impact of her wisdom and its profound influence on my character and actions.

As the seasons went by, life continued to test my resolve. There were days when I felt completely overwhelmed, ready to give in to the pressures around me. One evening, with my heart heavy, I confided in Momma. I shared my fears of failure and the harmful effects of going through a divorce. She responded with a gentle smile, sharing her own struggles and how her failed relationship before marrying my dad didn't stop her from being a mother or from giving God the glory. She reminded me that everything the devil meant for evil, God turned for good. Her faith in God sustained her through those difficult times. She told me that greatness lies within me and urged me not to lose hope.

"Keep being a phenomenal father, keep striving for greatness, keep making a positive difference in this world, and most importantly, keep the Lord in the midst of everything you do, and it will be impossible to fail." I learned from her to never give up and to maintain my faith through relentless prayer and sometimes fasting. "Whatever you do, do not ever give up, my dear," she urged, her conviction igniting a spark within me. "It's your faith that will carry you through."

I remember in 2013, my mom and I visited my dad's gravesite on his birthday, May 11th. That day, Momma emphasized the importance of not leaning on my own understanding but instead trusting in God's plan, even when it feels unclear. She discussed the importance of leaving a lasting legacy that begins within our families. "Plant seeds for the next generation," she insisted, her voice firm. "They are our greatest inheritance." It took time, but I came to understand that true legacy goes beyond material wealth; it's about nurturing love, passing down values, and sharing stories that last long after we're gone. She shared her love story with my dad and how powerful love truly is. She lamented how young people often struggle to experience faithful love because of how couples treat each other and how unforgiving people can be. She referenced 1 Corinthians, saying, "Love never fails."

She described what love looks like and said without hesitation, "Love is patient and kind; it is not jealous, does not boast, is not proud, and is not rude, baby. It is impossible to love without giving." When my mom shared her wisdom, she wanted me to understand its source, so she mentioned 1 Corinthians 13:8, which highlights that love is essential in life and faith. This passage states that no matter how gifted someone may be in speaking, understanding, or performing acts of charity, without love, those actions hold no value. It describes love as patient, kind, humble, and truthful, emphasizing that love endures all things and ultimately never fails. Meanwhile, other spiritual gifts and knowledge may eventually fade away. She also referenced John 3:16, saying that God so LOVED the world that He GAVE us His only Son. She wanted me to clearly understand that love and giving go hand in hand. She emphasized that she and my dad had true love for each other, and I witnessed that love firsthand.

Throughout my life, her words have often resonated with me, especially the mantra she would repeat: "Put your faith in the Lord, not in man, woman, or the government. It's God who sees your heart." This wisdom changed my perspective on life's disappointments and affirmed that while humans may fail me, God's purpose remains steadfast. From personal experience, I have learned that men can cheat you, women can con you, and the government can lie to you, but the Lord is faithful. His promises are guaranteed. The Bible tells us in Numbers 23:19, KJV, "God is not a man that He should lie; neither the son of man, that He should repent." This scripture confirms God's nature, showing that He is not fickle, biased, or inconsistent, but rather reliable and unmanipulable.

Years later, I found myself standing before my family at a gathering, with a blend of emotions swirling inside me. In that moment, I felt Momma's spirit woven into the very fabric of our lives. As I shared her stories and wisdom, a sense of peace hung over me. Her faithfulness, service, and purposeful life became my guiding principles.

As I finished my heartfelt speech, a deep realization settled in my heart: the true purpose of our lives is to strive to hear the Lord say, "Well done, good and faithful servant," and an entry through those golden gates. I understood that in those final moments of reflection, we think about the lives we've touched and the love we've shared. Momma Tyler embodied this calling. Her light still shines through me, nurturing the seeds she planted in my heart. I am committed to walking the path of faithful service, a testament to her lasting legacy, beautifully inspired.

My mom and dad both left a beautiful legacy—one of faith, compassion, resilience, family values, and the pursuit of a life that reflects love and service. These lessons will continue to be passed down through my children, inspiring them to embody these values in every aspect of their lives and to share them with future generations. I encourage you to apply these lessons to your own life and share them with your friends and family. Since you've reached the end, I know your wisdom has grown. I am very grateful and appreciative of your support.